HIP CHICK

TAROT

Maria Strom

REDFeather

MIND | BODY | SPIRIT

For all those who know and
will come to know the Tarot.

Type set in Spartan & Alba

ISBN: 978-0-7643-5492-2
Printed in China

Published by Schiffer Publishing, Ltd.
4880 Lower Valley Road
Atglen, PA 19310
Phone: (610) 593-1777; Fax: (610) 593-2002
E-mail: Info@schifferbooks.com
Web: www.schifferbooks.com

For our complete selection of fine books on this and related subjects, please visit our website at www.schifferbooks.com. You may also write for a free catalog.

Schiffer Publishing's titles are available at special discounts for bulk purchases for sales promotions or premiums. Special editions, including personalized covers, corporate imprints, and excerpts, can be created in large quantities for special needs. For more information, contact the publisher.

We are always looking for people to write books on new and related subjects. If you have an idea for a book, please contact us at proposals@schifferbooks.com.

CONTENTS

MAJOR ARCANA
Descriptions and Meanings . . . 29

MINOR ARCANA
Descriptions and Meanings ... 52

A MESSAGE FROM MARIA

Hip Chick Tarot is populated by strong women dealing with spiritual pursuits and life challenges. The colors are bold, and the symbols are modern and easy-to-read, making the deck accessible to both new and experienced readers.

Because I'm a woman and most of the people I read for are women, I created a deck for us. It's exciting and empowering to see women in cards that are usually held by men. And the messages of the cards are suited to our female psyche. Seeing my form in the cards and having the messages tailored to my experience helps me to absorb their meaning and apply it to my life. I hope *Hip Chick Tarot* does the same for you.

The women in this deck look like you and the women you know. We live in an increasingly diverse society, and I want *Hip Chick Tarot* to reflect that reality. I'm half Mexican and half Caucasian, so including all women is important to me, personally.

In more traditional decks, the suits are Wands, Cups, Swords, and Pentacles. I renamed them because I wanted to use language that's more contemporary. All the suits have many aspects but, given the challenge of using just one word to express each, I chose: Create (traditionally Wands) represented by a paintbrush, Feel (traditionally Cups) represented by a heart, Think (traditionally Swords) represented by a light bulb, and Earth (traditionally Pentacles) represented by a world.

Each card is hand-painted. I placed the women on solid backgrounds, using heavy outlines to give them the timeless quality of icons.

Having distinct colors for each suit helps make reading easier. With a quick glance at a spread, you can pick up on a dominant color that relates to a particular suit and know that energy is elevated in the reading.

Red represents Create because it's fiery and passionate. Blue is the color of water, the element associated with emotions, so it represents Feel. Yellow is for Think because it's associated with the illumination that thoughts can bring. And brown, the color of the land, stands for Earth. The Major Arcana is represented by the color purple because purple is recognized as a highly spiritual color.

A few easy-to-read symbols are seen throughout the deck:

Suns indicate external energy, blessings, self-realization, and joy.

Smiley Faces indicate happiness.

Moons represent internal energy and mystery.

Clouds can mean heaviness, sadness, challenges, or mystery.

Water stands for emotions and flow.

Mountains represent higher awareness.

Owls symbolize wisdom.

Plants are about growth and bringing something into fruition.

Flowers, in general, are about beauty. Daisies, in particular, are about the beauty found in simplicity.

I chose a daisy for the back of each card because daisies are unassuming, yet lovely; they're just as comfortable growing along a roadside as they are being admired in a vase. I believe the Tarot teaches us that beauty is all around us, especially in the simplest things.

Some of the Major Arcana have been renamed to reflect modern, everyday vocabulary and concepts, but the energies portrayed are similar to those found in traditional decks:

Empress is Nature.
Emperor is Structure.
Hierophant is Sacred Knowledge.
Chariot is Will.
Wheel of Fortune is just Wheel.
Hanged Man is Hangin'.
Temperance is Flow.

Devil is Bound.
Judgment is Reborn.
World is Universe.

Hip Chick Tarot is here to assist you in your spiritual development and help you navigate through the ups and downs of your life. The Major Arcana (the twenty-two purple cards) are the heavy hitters of the spiritual arena, and if a lot of them show up in your reading, a lot of inner change is happening. The cards may clarify the changes occurring in your psyche or point to a new consciousness that's on your horizon, or they may simply assure you that you're on the right path.

The Minor Arcana (the fifty-six cards representing the suits of Create, Feel, Think, and Earth) tend to deal with the stuff of life: your creativity and passion, your feelings and relationships, your thoughts and struggles, your work, and your health.

The descriptions of the Major Arcana include interpretations for both spiritual and practical situations. Even though the deck is divided into the Major and Minor cards, there's no rigid boundary. You're a spiritual being living in the material world, so your spirituality is developed not just in quiet reflection, study, and meditation, but through your experiences of everyday life. All the cards point to the final card of the Major Arcana, the Divine manifest in the Universe—which is a state of non-duality, where the spiritual/material, inner/outer merge—and move to the beat of life.

MAJOR ARCANA

In pure form, the Major Arcana shows you the elements of your inner world. The cards express archetypes, and you recognize them because you see yourself in them and you resonate with their spiritual and psychological truth. You—you fabulous Divine Being—are so vast and wonderful that you contain all twenty-two of these potentialities within yourself! While the potential of each card is unique, they all assist you in connecting to an aspect of your Divinity and point out the most positive, powerful way to use it.

There's a path of spiritual development that starts with the innocence and courage of the Fool and moves to the wisdom and liberation of the Universe. But the journey isn't always linear. As you get to know the Major Arcana, you may see yourself moving through the different energies these cards represent, and you may find that you jump around or take a detour on the path. You may seem to be stuck and then—all of a sudden—you leap ahead or go back to revisit an archetypical lesson. Remember: It's all good, unfolding the way it should.

Major Arcana energies can also help with life's everyday problems. For example, Hangin' could show up in a reading to reflect a spiritual shift, a time of going within and changing the way you view life. Or, if the reading is about a conflict you're having with someone, Hangin' might be calling you to see the problem from the other person's point of view.

MINOR ARCANA

The four suits of the Minor Arcana are about the day-to-day reality of your life. These cards remind you that all of your life is sacred. Your body, your relationships, your work, your joys and struggles, and all the experiences that come your way are valuable.

These suit cards guide you through minor dilemmas and major changes—from how to take better care of yourself to making a decision about whether or not to take a job that's located across the country.

While the Major Arcana deals more with big spiritual shifts, your spirituality is played out in your daily life; that's the realm of the majority of the deck, the fifty-six cards of the Minor Arcana. The biggest spiritual epiphany can manifest in something as small as the patience you show the barista who's just learning how to make a cappuccino or the coworker who's going on too long in a meeting. The suit cards help you tune into your feelings, think positively, be creative, and stay grounded.

As you work with the cards and grow spiritually, you become aware of how your inner and outer worlds merge. The labels "good" and "bad" fall away because you value all of your experiences. That's what Create, Feel, Think, and Earth cards represent: the messy, glorious experience of life!

FAMILY CARDS

The Court Cards in a traditional deck are King, Queen, Knight, and Page. *Hip Chick Tarot* cards are: Queen, Boss, Teen, and Child. I see this group of women as a family. Queens are very spiritually evolved. Next come Bosses with their ability to organize and get stuff done. Teens are impulsive, but they contribute lots of energy and enthusiasm. And Child cards represent the essence, innocence, and spontaneity of each suit.

This group of women and girls show up in your readings with something to tell you; think of them as BFFs who've got your best interest at heart, the kind of friends who are always there to listen to you and give you solid advice. Each one has her own personality that's influenced by her suit. You tend to draw the friend who has the energy you're working with or you need to put to use.

The women in the Create group are creative and energetic. The women in the Feel group work in the realm of relationships and emotions. The women in the Think group are curious and intellectual. And the women in the Earth group tend to be practical and grounded. Their messages may be encouraging or cautionary, depending on the situation and the other cards surrounding them.

HOW TO USE HIP CHICK TAROT

Simply shuffling the cards and laying out a spread is an act of faith. It's a way to acknowledge your connection to the Universe and the Divine energy that flows through you and manifests in the cards you choose. The cards that appear in your spread are the ones meant to be there.

Working with the Tarot opens you up, expands your awareness, and engages your intuition. When I get a good reading, I feel like my world view widens enough to see beyond my immediate concerns; I crack open a little (or a lot) and life force comes flooding in. It's exhilarating, encouraging, and mysterious because that's what life is really like!

It's up to you to find your own way of reading the Tarot, but I'll share the way I read in order to give you some ideas: After I lay out a spread, I scan the cards and pick up on colors, numbers, images, and feelings. If I see a lot of blue backgrounds, for example, I know the suit of Feel is predominate and relationships and feelings are playing a big role in the reading. Numbers are also informative. For example, if a lot of fours show up in a reading that could indicate stability or, perhaps, rigidity.

The cards come together to create a narrative, and I'm guided to tell that story. There's a three-way energy between the cards, the client, and me. What I'm feeling, what I feel from the client, and what I get from the cards all inform the reading.

When you read for yourself, a feeling of connection develops between you and the cards, and your intuition informs your reading. It's best to do it when you're calm and relaxed so you can hear what the cards are trying to tell you. That can be a challenge when you're seeking guidance about something that's bothering you. You may be eager to hear what the cards have to say, but remember: Their message comes through clearest when it doesn't have to be filtered through your anxiety. Find a way to comfort and calm yourself and come to the cards with an open heart.

It's possible to interpret the same card in a different way each time it appears in a spread. For example, the Child of Think might mean thinking outside the box to solve a problem in one reading and another time it may mean having fun or working with children or thinking about having a child. It depends on the question being asked and the cards surrounding it.

You don't need to worry about memorizing the meanings of each card. You can simply "read" the pictures and look up the descriptions when you feel you need more clarification. My hope is, as you become familiar with the deck, your intuition flows into your readings, and you feel increasingly comfortable to interpret the cards in a way that feels natural to you.

SPIRITUAL GROWTH, EVERYDAY LIFE, AND THE CARDS

The Tarot provides wisdom, guidance, and affirmation. The seventy-eight cards and all their possible combinations are here to help you deal with just about anything you're going through. You can consult the Tarot about your internal life; it can guide you and affirm you through shifts in your consciousness. Or you can ask the Divine to channel wisdom through the cards to help you with events in your life, such as dealing with a breakup or handling an issue at work.

All the cards are spiritual because all your issues, all your feelings, and all your daily joys and challenges are part of your spiritual path.

Often your issues, the tough stuff you inherited from your childhood and the unprocessed traumatic experiences you've encountered throughout your life, are portals into spirituality. As you bring these experiences into conscious awareness, you connect to deep places within. You feel and then release the pain stored there. This process allows you to truly know yourself and care for yourself.

Healing is a spiritual journey that opens your heart and expands your consciousness. Often, despite the pain, people come to view their issues as teachers and embrace the lessons they bring. For instance, a client of mine had a really cold mother. And the dysfunction in her family made it difficult for her to connect with other family members, too. Because her family of origin was unable to give her the love and support that she needed, she turned to the Divine within her for that support. This connection has been there to guide and comfort her throughout her life. In retrospect, she views the loneliness and pain her family gave her as part of her process. Her connection to the Divine gives her life meaning and direction. She's an authentic person, and she knows how to nurture herself and the people she's chosen to be in her life.

Some cards, like Hermit, call you to go inside, while other cards, like Will, are about acting in the world. The Flow card represents the end of inner/outer duality and celebrates the merging of your internal life with your daily life rooted on planet Earth.

As you respond with love to all the happenings of your life, even the stuff that's challenging, you feel comfortable and relaxed. You watch your need to control slip away. As you become enlightened (and yes, you can be enlightened because it's not some mysterious state; it's just your natural self), you know the meaning of the Universe card.

The woman in the Universe card isn't spinning her hula-hoop in a monastery or on a mountaintop; she's twirling it through her daily life. She recognizes the Divine in her morning coffee and her hands curled around the cup. She sees it in the litter box that needs to be cleaned and the inbox full of email that's waiting for her reply. She recognizes the same Divine energy in her irritable client and her loving spouse.

Because you're a spiritual being living here on earth, all the way through your spiritual path you'll be dealing with daily-life stuff. That's where the Zen saying applies: "Before enlightenment, chop wood, carry water. After enlightenment, chop wood, carry water." So, after you experience the truth of the Universe card, you'll still be doing the same stuff—washing dishes, taking out the trash, writing computer code, and mountain biking, for example—only you'll be doing it with an enlightened spirit.

All the cards are here to help you, but there will be ones that really jump out as you develop spirituality. They're different for everyone and change over time. At one point in my journey, Tower really resonated with me. Tower power acknowledged the breaking up of my old patterns of fear and rigidity.

Doing internal work was difficult, sometimes, and even scary, because after I cleared away the old stuff, I was left with a void for a while until I grew into my new consciousness. The Hangin' card helped me to acknowledge these times in my life and to stay calm and patient.

There was a point when Flow started showing up all the time, in almost every reading I did for myself, to acknowledge my experience of inner and outer merging. At that point in my life, I was in awe of all the synchronicity and magic I was experiencing.

Experiencing synchronicity and receiving signs and signals is amazing and reassuring. But these bursts of energy are accompanied by longer periods of integration. After all that magic and excitement, it's important to remember that the "boring" parts, the everyday-life stuff, is where you practice your amazing gift of Divine connection. What good is it if you receive awe-inspiring signals from the Universe and you can't be patient with yourself or simply take the time to listen to a friend?

NO "BAD" CARDS AND NO "BAD" FEELINGS

The cards acknowledge your feelings, and they invite you to acknowledge them, too. Given the choice, you'd probably rather be feeling the joy of Sun and the stability of Four of Earth than the moodiness of Moon and the confusion of Seven of Feel.

You might have learned to value some of your feelings over others. Do you ever find yourself disowning anger or jealously, for example? Do you feel that spiritual people aren't supposed to feel that way? Well, *Hip Chick Tarot* is telling you that your feelings—all your feelings—are valuable. There are no orphan feelings in *Hip Chick Tarot* because all feelings belong.

Your feelings change; none of them lasts forever, but when they're with you, they want to be comfortable. So, why not be a good host and welcome them by name? Hello Anger, I see you and I love you. What can I get you? A pillow to beat up on? A cup of tea? Some soothing music?

Acknowledging and loving your feelings is acknowledging and loving your humanity. It's expansive energy, and it leads to compassion for yourself, and that compassion spreads to others. Instead of feeling irritated with a feeling, get comfortable with it. The funny thing is: Just as soon as your feeling feels comfy, it gets ready to go on its way, confident to return when it needs to, but usually with a little less intensity.

REVERSALS

Reverse meanings are not included. I don't work with reversals in my practice, but I acknowledge that many readers do. A reversed *Hip Chick Tarot* card can be interpreted to have the same energy as one that's upright, just to a lesser degree.

FAVORITE SPREADS

Here are some spreads to get you on your way. The Celtic Cross is tried-and-true and loved throughout the Tarot community. I've included a few that I created, too: Three-Card Soul Dive Spread, Six-Card Relationship Spread, and Four-Card Project Spread. You can use these, find more on the Internet, or make up your own. I really encourage you to make up your own—it's fun and a great way to identify what you're looking for from the cards.

CELTIC CROSS SPREAD

The Celtic Cross spread is the one I usually use for clients and for myself when I need a reading that's comprehensive, powerful, and clear. This spread is a classic; it's probably the most well-known and most used. I learned it back when I was a teenager, and I've been using it ever since.

The spread gets its name because the cards are placed in a Circle/Cross pattern that resembles the Celtic Cross symbol that goes back to the early Middle Ages. According to popular legend in Ireland, the Christian Cross was joined with the circle representing the sun god, melding early Roman Christianity with the pagan beliefs of the Celts.

In addition to the six cards that form the circle/cross, there are four more cards stacked to the right of it. Reading them from the bottom to the top, they represent the path from unconsciousness to consciousness.

10 Outcome

Eight of Feel

9 Hopes and Fears

Ace of Earth

5 Crown

Two of Earth

4 Behind   **1 Present**   **6 Before**

2 Cross   Teen of Earth

Queen of Think

Three of Create

High Priestess

8 Environment

Tower

3 Foundation

Seven of Earth

7 You

Strength

Card 1: Present

What's happening now? This card represents what the reading is about; it's the heart of the situation you're exploring.

Card 2: Cross

What crosses you? This card is placed over the "Present" Card. It brings more information to the situation you're examining. It can magnify the energy of the "Present" card, be in opposition to it, or offer a whole new angle.

Card 3: Foundation

Appropriately, this card forms the bottom of the cross, the foundation. It's a soulful card representing the source of the situation, the unconscious and deeper meaning.

Card 4: Behind

The "Behind" card represents the energy that's fading. This energy may have influenced the situation, but it's being replaced by new energy found in the "Crown" and "Before" cards.

Card 5: Crown

Whereas the "Foundation" card is the card of the unconscious, the "Crown" card is the card of the conscious. It represents what you believe to be true about the situation, what you want and your goals.

Card 6: Before

This is the card that represents the way the energy is moving. Because it's in the future, you have the ability to work with it, to influence it.

Card 7: You

This card is all about you; it may be representing how you see yourself or how you wish to be seen. It can represent what you bring to the situation, such as a talent or an insight or, perhaps, a blind spot.

Card 8: Environment

This card represents the opinions and influence of the people in your life regarding the matter. It may point to the benefits of seeking counsel from friends and family, or it might be signaling that it's best to keep your own counsel.

Card 9: Hopes and Fears

The card in the "Hopes and Fears" position, the one right before "Outcome," has a lot to say. In addition to offering your deepest feelings about the matter, it can sometimes offer guidance about how you can proceed. It may bring up something overlooked or unexpected that you'll want to consider.

Card 10: Outcome

This card indicates the way things are likely to go. The "Outcome" card can also suggest the lesson to be learned from the experience.

Celtic Cross Spread Sample Reading

My client asked, "I want to know about my business. Will things get better?" After she shuffled, I fanned the deck out in front of her and instructed her to pick ten cards, focusing on the placement of each one: The first card she chose was for the "Present" position; the second for the "Cross" position; the third for "Foundation," and so on.

I scanned the spread for an overall sense of what was going on. What I picked up on right away was that four out of the ten cards were from the Earth suit (that made sense since the question was about business). The next thing I noticed was that in the "Present" position was the Three of Create card "crossed" by Teen of Earth. It was about taking the first step forward (Three of Create) and how difficult that would be (Teen of Earth).

Seven of Earth in the "Foundation" spot pointed in the same direction; she had reached a pause point where a decision needed to be made in order to move forward. In the "Crown" position was Two of Earth, pointing out the importance of regaining balance. Queen of Think in the "Behind" position and High Priestess in the "Before" position was really interesting to me; my interpretation was that my client had moved from scrutinizing the situation and being angry about it to going within and connecting to her higher self in order to handle it.

Tower (a really explosive card) in the "Environment" position stressed the magnitude of the situation. When I asked if the problem involved someone at work, she said yes and explained that it was a manager—and someone who had become a close friend—not just an employee.

My client looked sad and discouraged as she told me how she could no longer trust her friend's judgment and that the business had suffered because of her friend's decisions. I nodded and pointed to the Tower card and told her how it was affirming her feelings: The situation at work had reached a crisis level.

Then I focused on the need to take action and acknowledged how difficult that was by pointing to the Teen of Earth card (the young woman weighed down by the world). We both agreed that a decision was difficult, but needed to be made. It just couldn't be put off any longer! She had to let this woman go and, most likely, from her life as well as from her business; chances were slim that the friendship could survive the dismal situation.

I turned her attention to Strength in the "You" position and congratulated her on her ability to handle this really tough situation. I reassured her by pointing out Ace of Earth in the "Hopes and Fears" position. Deep down, she already knew that everything was going to get better.

The "Outcome" card really summed it up—Eight of Feel— leaving something (or someone in this case) behind in order to move on.

THREE·CARD SOUL DIVE SPREAD

You can use this simple three-card spread to take a dive into your soul; it's a snapshot of what's going on with you on a deeper level. I use it to acknowledge how what I'm going through relates to the bigger picture of my life: how me, my current circumstances, and my spirituality are connected.

Often, this spread helps me grow and learn from what the Universe is presenting me. And it helps me acknowledge my feelings and take care of myself.

3 Soul Connection

Will

1 You

Queen of Earth

2 What's Happening

Six of Think

Card 1: You
The first card represents you at this time, your inner state, how you can care for yourself.

Card 2: What's Happening
The second card represents the experience the Universe is bringing to you.

Card 3: Soul Connection
The third card represents your deepest self, what's evolving to help you grow.

Soul Dive
Spread Sample Reading

I did this reading for myself at a time when I was changing. I could feel it. Everything had slowed down. I stopped socializing, preferring to spend my time alone. I didn't want to do much at all. I spent my free time going for walks or just hanging out on the couch with my cats. I knew from previous internal shifts that another one was happening and that it was important. Yet, I felt weird about withdrawing from people (I had just moved and was getting to know new people;

23

was I missing out?), and what was all this leading to anyway?

Queen of Earth was in the "Me" position, so I asked myself what she'd do if she were in my shoes. The answer was, of course—take care of herself and do what feels comfortable and right. Her message was so reassuring—thank you Queen of Earth!

Six of Think in the "What's Happening" position pointed to my transition and what I was feeling: I was changing the way I viewed myself and the world. I was moving on, leaving behind an old way of being.

Will in the "Soul" position addressed the conflict I felt lurking around. I was torn between my soul's desire to change and the tug of my social life. Will is about acknowledging the conflict, choosing a course of action, and moving forward, despite fears.

This reading helped me make the decision to leave relationships and activities behind (at least for a while) in order to go deeper, know myself better, and direct my energy into what benefited me the most. I needed some alone time to integrate the lessons I was learning. Another layer of my people-pleasing behaviors was falling away; it felt heavy and dishonest, and I didn't want to carry it around anymore. It was time to take care of me!

This reading helped me acknowledge the sadness I was feeling about letting go of relationships and the fear of moving forward into a new, unfamiliar way of being. And it encouraged me to do it anyway.

SIX-CARD RELATIONSHIP SPREAD

This spread can help when there's an issue going on in a relationship, any kind of relationship; it can be with a spouse, partner, family member, friend, coworker, boss, or even a group or institution.

And the issue doesn't have to be about conflict; it can stand for a goal you're working toward or whatever else fits your situation. The purpose of this reading is to clarify why you and the other are connecting, what you're working toward, and what you can share.

1 You   **2 What You Bring**   **5 Issue**   **3 Other Person**   **4 What They Bring**

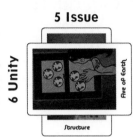

6 Unity

Ace of Create   Six of Create   Structure   Five of Earth   Eight of Earth   Seven of Earth

Card 1: You
This card represents you at this time: your attitudes, beliefs and desires.

Card 2: What You Bring
This card represents what you have to contribute: your positivity and strengths as well as your doubts and weaknesses.

Card 3: Other Person (or group)
This card represents the other person at this time: their attitudes, beliefs, and desires.

Card 4: What They Bring
This card represents what they have to contribute: their positivity and strengths as well as their doubts and weaknesses.

Card 5: Issue
This card represents what both parties share or have been brought together to experience.

Card 6: Unity
This card is about the energy that can unite both people. It expresses what you can acknowledge or move toward in order to create a positive experience.

Relationship Spread Sample Reading

I did this reading for a woman who asked me, "Will my relationship with my wife improve?"

A quick glance at this spread told me that the two women were committed to the relationship, and it was built on solid ground. My client in the "You" position was represented by Ace of Create—what an optimistic card—and Six of Create, representing what she contributes took that optimism even further. She had lots of energy and positivity to put into the relationship.

Her wife was hard working and committed as shown by Eight of Earth, although perhaps a little perfectionistic. She may be coming from a place of re-evaluating something and wanting to make some changes (Seven of Earth).

Structure in the "Issue" position pointed to a solid foundation. The "Unity" card was Five of Earth. When I asked her if she'd been feeling disconnected from her wife, my client said yes. They weren't spending much time together; her wife was worried about her job and didn't seem to have much energy to put into the relationship. I could see that was in direct opposition to the tremendous energy that my client was bringing to the relationship—she really wanted to make this better!

I pointed out that she and her wife shared Five of Earth energy, a feeling of uncertainty, but for different reasons: her wife was experiencing it at work, and she was experiencing it through her relationship with her wife.

I advised her to give her wife the emotional space necessary for her to focus on the work issue. I assured her there was no need to worry; the relationship was stable and could weather this storm.

FOUR·CARD PROJECT SPREAD

This spread provides a quick take on career and projects. I've used it when I'm struggling on a project or wondering if I should take on a new freelance gig.

4 Action

Two of Earth

1 Project

2 You

Fool

Strength

3 Environment

Three of Think

Card 1: Project
The first card represents the project or job.

Card 2: You
The second card represents what you bring to the project or job. This can be your attitude, skills, or experience—whatever you're contributing that's most influencing the work at this time.

Card 3: Environment
This card is about the workplace environment. It can represent how your coworkers and boss influence how you feel and what you're working on, or it can represent how you feel about your home office or workspace.

Card 4: Action

This is the course of action that will help you and your work succeed.

Project Spread Sample Reading

I felt the need to do a project spread when I first started working as a freelance copywriter. There were challenges (I'd never done this kind of work before and needed to do some extra research in order to make up for my inexperience), but I felt confident I could handle it, and Strength in the "Project" position validated my feelings.

In the "Me" position was Fool, and I laughed when I pulled it. I knew I was a little over my head when I took this project on, but I had decided to do it anyway.

The "Environment" card was Three of Think and that got me in touch with the fact that I wasn't having any fun. It felt kind of weird because I had been wanting to work from home, and I had worked hard to get the assignment.

When I thought about it, I realized I missed people, and I didn't like being in my apartment all day. As much as I liked not having to get dressed and go to the office, I was starting to feel isolated, and I was questioning my decision to be a freelancer.

The "Action" card was Two of Earth. Of course—I needed to bring some balance to my work life. I decided that meant leaving the apartment more. I slipped my computer in my backpack and hit the town.

At first, I just went to a local cafe to work. Then, I started traveling to other parts of the city, really making an adventure out of the outings. After I did a few hours of research and writing, I'd take a break and, sometimes, check out an exhibit at a museum or walk in a park. A few times, I met a friend for lunch; even if I didn't have coworkers, I could be around other people.

The reading helped me recognize my need to take advantage of my situation instead of feeling limited by it. I used my flexible work schedule to build variety and fun into my days. Going out breathed new life into the work, and I ended up really enjoying it.

MAJOR ARCANA DESCRIPTIONS AND MEANINGS

FOOL

Fool

Description
This woman is taking off with nothing more than a suitcase and a sense of adventure. Her roller skates symbolize youth, and the smiley face symbolizes happiness. She's hitchhiking because she's trusting and unaware of danger. The road behind her twists and turns; she doesn't know where she's going, and it doesn't matter—it's not about the destination, it's about the journey!

Spiritual
Traditional ways of thinking give way to a whole new outlook. This process may seem disorienting because there are times when the old slips, and the new hasn't completely arrived, and you seem to be experiencing a profound nothingness. This Divine nothingness takes you deep into self, into soul.

Fool energy is innocent and trusting and keenly aware of its dependence on the Divine. You don't have all the answers and that's okay. It's about ah-ha moments and then stumbling and getting back up, like learning to walk. And it's all good—fools are protected by angels!

Practical
Fool energy can pop up in your life in exciting ways, urging you to break out of a rut and live life fully. You may feel the pull to move to a foreign country or leave a job or take the leap into a new relationship.

The movement that beckons bubbles up from your unconscious; it comes from feeling, not thinking and planning. Often, there are key moments in life, when the time is right for change, and you hear the call of the Fool. It's wise to follow.

CREATOR

Creator

Description

Creator is surrounded by the symbols of the Minor Arcana (light bulb, heart, paintbrush, and earth) because she uses all that's available to her: her thoughts, feelings, creativity, and skill to take her Divine vision and turn it into reality.

Spiritual

Creator's power comes from knowing how to use energy—Divine energy—in the world. Moving on from the unconscious state of Fool, Creator is wide awake and fully aware of the energy stream available to her.

By being calm, letting your ego take a backseat, and opening up your heart, you can welcome in this powerful creative energy. Ideas and solutions will come to you, but the intensity may scare you, and you may hide from it by worrying or bingeing on food or spending too much time online or whatever your distraction of choice may be. But fear not, Creator is here with this message: You don't have to hold on to this powerful energy—it's meant to be directed and released into the world. Think of yourself as a channel with Divine energy flowing through you into your creation. Go ahead—be bold—take what's possible and turn it into what's real!

Practical

Success is achieved by claiming your power, harnessing your will, and moving toward your goal. If you have begun a new project, pulling Creator is a reminder that you have what it takes to see your project to fruition.

HIGH PRIESTESS

High Priestess

Description

This beautiful woman pulls back the veil, inviting you to go inside and connect to your soul. Her third eye is well developed; she's able to see beyond the physical into spiritual truth. The moon, representing the unconscious, floats above her head. She sits comfortably between two cats, a black one symbolizing darkness and a white one symbolizing light.

Spiritual

High Priestess realizes one of the most profound truths of the Tarot—that deep understanding is inside of you. You already sense it through your intuition and by glimpsing the synchronicity that's always lurking around.

This knowledge lies outside of the rational knowledge that most people think is running things, but High Priestess knows better. And she's here to invite you to know too—to pull back the thin veil that everybody calls "reality" and see the real reality—that the Divine lives inside of you and connects you to everyone and everything.

Meditation and other spiritual pursuits can help you on this journey, but remember: You already have this knowledge—you just need to let it come to the surface of your consciousness. As High Priestess leads you on the spiritual path, your intuition blossoms, and the Universe sends you signals. Enjoy this beautiful unfolding.

Practical

In more practical matters, High Priestess points out the potential not yet realized in the situation. You may need to look deeper to see the possibilities in your relationships and endeavors. This card is not about the seen, but the unseen. Use your intuition.

ΠΛTUR€

Παture

Description

This chick is in tune with all that surrounds her. She wades in water with vines growing around her arm and birds nesting in her hair. She's part of nature, and she harnesses the power of "go with the flow." The flowers represent her beauty, and the lightning represents her power.

Spiritual

Nature is life. She's expansive, sexual—and spiritual—and you are, too! A lot of us were taught to separate the spiritual from the material, but hey, all of life is infused with Spirit, and that's what Nature wants you to remember. Your bellybutton is a manifestation of the Divine, so is your appendix scar, and your earlobe. The sex you had last night and the eggs that you're eating for breakfast this morning are all part of the Divine.

You and everyone and everything else on this planet are governed by the laws of nature and the cycles of life and death. Your power lies in using your intuition and flowing with life. When the Nature card shows up, she's calling you to see the big picture, remember your passion, claim your power—and love your life!

Practical

Nature energy helps in all arenas of life because it calls you to relax and let life happen. If you're a writer feeling stuck, stop forcing it and come back to the project, naturally, when the time is right. If you're a mom feeling frustrated, Nature reminds you to remember life's stages and to be patient with yourself and your child.

∫TRUCTURE

Structure

Description

This chick knows how to get it done! Her crown shows her accomplishment, and the books on her head represent her knowledge. The plane overhead represents the high goals she sets for herself. The pencil and ruler represent her practicality, and the people on their way to work represent her management skills. But there's a deeper, spiritual meaning to Structure: Her lesson involves applying boundaries and discipline to access Divine energy.

Spiritual

Spirituality requires the use of Structure energies, such as limitation, discipline, and focus. Artists are keenly aware of how limitation releases their creativity; the blank canvas is overwhelming, so the artist picks a subject and focuses on it, eliminating countless other options. The very process of elimination frees her to express her creativity. It's a paradox, limitation inviting expansion.

Often spiritual growth requires this energy; through meditation, focusing and limiting thought, you experience expansion of consciousness. Simply, being kind and respectful to others requires discipline. It can be hard to hold back a snarky remark from someone who's being rude or refrain from yelling at your spouse during a heated argument. Focusing on the big, expansive spiritual picture requires discipline when you feel frustrated with the daily-life stuff.

Practical

Structure shows up to help you focus and apply yourself. Whether your goal is going to the gym or starting a new business, you need discipline to succeed. Structure is there to anchor your imagination and creativity to the real world—it's the foundation for your dreams.

SACRED KNOWLEDGE

Sacred Knowledge

Description
This spiritual teacher is surrounded by sacred symbols. Her book is marked with a spiral that stands for growth and evolution. Her hat is shaped like a fish, an early Christian symbol. The ancient Egyptian ankh simply means "life." The Buddhist lotus stands for purity. And the snake symbolizes transformation.

Spiritual
As you walk your spiritual path, you'll crave sacred knowledge and wisdom. Generations of enlightened people have recorded their messages for you. A book or a video can affirm your feelings and deepen your spiritual understanding. A workshop or a retreat may resonate with you. Or, maybe, sharing your experiences with others in a religious community or spiritual group would be helpful.

You might have received religious instruction as a child and that might have been helpful or it might have been harmful. As a spiritual seeker and as an adult—now, you have the choice— to pick what tradition or what traditions can assist you on your spiritual path.

Practical
Knowledge is power—so Sacred Knowledge helps you practically, too. It'll usually show up directing you to go deeper into the matter, study, or seek outside council. Say your spread is about taking a trip to South America; Sacred Knowledge may appear, advising you not to wing it, to read some guide books, and talk to other travelers before you hop on the plane. The message is: You don't need to reinvent the wheel—access the information available and learn from others.

LOVERS

Lovers

Description
Lovers unite in a kiss while the sun above radiates blessings. They each sport heart tattoos, symbols of their love and passion.

Spiritual
Mystics have described their union with God in terms of sexual ecstasy. When you surrender yourself fully in intimacy with another, you drop your social mask, your ego slips, and duality disappears. You and your partner unite, if just for a moment. That passionate spiritual connection is what this card is about.

Lovers asks you to choose—choose what your heart deeply desires—because that's the path to an authentic life. That decision could be choosing a person to love. Or choosing to unite with the Divine. The choice could be to connect to a career that energizes you and harnesses your passion.

What you choose is not the point—only that it's your calling. It takes a tremendous amount of courage to follow your own path and not be swayed by society's messages and the opinions of others. Lovers is here to tell you: Don't take your life for granted—embrace the responsibility of living it honestly and passionately.

Practical
It's about choosing connection over isolation. Lovers may encourage you to get to know someone or risk going deeper in a relationship or activity you love.

It can point to good feelings among people, in your workplace, in your family, or other social spaces. It's a sign you can trust others and feel comfortable with them.

WILL

Will

Description

The Will woman sports a sun-god halo representing her power. She walks two cats on leashes, one black and one white. The cats symbolize conflicting thoughts and feelings that are skillfully kept under the woman's control in order for her to move forward.

Spiritual

Everyone knows cats are hard to control. How is she able to do it? By applying her will. The Will card is here to help you claim your power and surrender your power. A contradiction, right? Well, the woman in this card is a master at dealing with contradictions. She wants you to be able to handle conflicting thoughts and feelings and move forward. You do this by making decisions—the best decisions you can—while acknowledging you're mortal and don't have all the answers. Then you make plans and put them into action.

The key is surrendering the outcome to the Divine. That's the point when you drop the leashes, let the cats go, and don't look back. This process is empowering because you're doing your part, the Universe is doing its thing, and you're letting go of fear and worry. That's partnering with the Divine!

Practical

When Will shows up in your reading, it usually indicates success. It reminds you that you have what it takes to control your fear, move forward and achieve—despite any obstacle! And it reminds you that your failures are to be embraced, too. It's all part of the journey. Keep going and you'll get there.

STRENGTH

Strength

Description

Glancing at the woman in this card, you don't necessarily think "strength"; that's because her strength is internal. She's strong enough to be naked and vulnerable in the presence of the tiger who symbolizes challenging feelings. The mountain in the background represents higher awareness, and the sun speaks of self-realization.

Spiritual

Controlling your feelings helps you function and be socially acceptable, but to really know yourself requires giving your feelings some acceptance and space. Instead of denying her anger and shoving it into a cage, the naked woman is strong enough to be vulnerable and gently soothe it. By making her anger feel comfortable, the tiger's roar softens to a purr.

Your compulsions, unwanted habits, and negative feelings can be frustrating. Like a tangled knot that grows tighter each time you pull, they require skill and patience to unravel. The woman in the Strength card doesn't fight or run. She sits with the tiger and tames it through love. Strength invites you to truly love yourself—all of yourself—even the parts you have labeled undesirable. You are being asked to use your strength to go inside and befriend and tame your demons.

Practical

The Strength card has shown up in your reading to reassure you that you have the resources to face your problems and handle them. Strength encourages you to be honest with yourself and take care of yourself by finding the calm inside of you, so you can make your best move forward.

HERMIT

Hermit

Description

Hermit sits cross-legged in her cave. The cave represents the underground or unconscious aspects of herself that she's bringing to light. Alone, in the darkness, her inner light, represented by the candle she holds, burns brightly, guiding her on her inward journey. Above her head, a tree grows, symbolizing knowledge, and the owl perched in it symbolizes wisdom.

Spiritual

Hermit calls you to withdraw from the outer world to focus on inner development. Society values the extrovert out there mixin' it up and gettin' it done, so answering Hermit's call requires courage.

During this sensitive time, you may receive guidance from a teacher, someone who has walked the inner path of development, but often your own psyche is the guide. By eliminating distractions and cultivating calm, you're able to connect to your psyche; you give it respect and space and let it speak to you.

In this state, the Divine supports you by sending signs and symbols to affirm your journey. Maybe when you check the time it shows repeating numbers, for example, 1:11 or 4:44. A bird may suddenly appear on your windowsill when you're graced with an illuminating thought, and your dreams may become more vivid, meaningful, and memorable.

For some, this card may indicate that you're ready to take on the role of spiritual teacher and share what you've learned.

Practical

In practical matters, Hermit advises you not to listen to the counsel of others, but to tune into yourself for the answers.

WHEEL

Wheel

Description
The woman stands in the center of the wheel, poised and ready to roll.

Spiritual
Wheel symbolizes external events in your life—the ups, downs, and in-be-tweens—but the spiritual lesson is found inside of you. By holding her center inside (not projecting it out there on other people and circumstances), the woman in the Wheel card remains calm as she rolls with her life.

She's the hub of her wheel. She enjoys being on top, but she doesn't need everything going her way to be happy. And she isn't dependent on the approval of others. Why should she be? She knows her value. When the wheel hits bottom, she doesn't despair; she's confident in her ability to handle it.

So, the question is: How do *you* roll? When you pull the Wheel card, you're being asked to be the hub of your wheel. By focusing on the Divine within, you can be calm (or pretty close to it) in almost any situation. And with calm comes comfort to get you through the tough times. Calm brings composure, too, so you don't get carried away when it's all going great.

Practical
Wheel indicates change, usually something big. It can be a new job or the loss of a job, a clean bill of health or the news that you need surgery. Whatever's happening, Wheel reminds you that the nature of life is change. One day you're on top, the next day you're on the bottom. But wait . . . you're headed to the top again!

JUSTICE

Justice

Description

The woman in this card sits in the now, between the wilting rose and the rose bud, representing past and future. From this middle ground, she calls you to consciously examine your past in order to create a better future. Above her are the scales of justice, symbolizing your need to weigh your actions according to your own values and to account for them.

Spiritual

Justice is the "get real" card. This process requires that you're vigorously honest with yourself, owning how you have hurt yourself and others. The next step is self-forgiveness.

It's also a good time to release the pain others have inflicted on you. This isn't always easy; you may need to work with a therapist or perform forgiveness rituals to be able to let go of this pent-up energy.

By accepting all that has happened, the happy times and the painful parts as well—you accept yourself and your life—and you become free. You're able to move forward, releasing the weight of the past and taking with you the wisdom and knowledge you've gained from it. You can direct your future with good decisions and right action.

Practical

In practical matters, Justice encourages you to walk your talk—to be honest and fair to yourself and others in all your dealings.

Regarding a particular situation, and depending on the surrounding cards, Justice may either show up to let you know you can trust someone or indicate you should withhold your trust.

HANGIN'

Hangin'

Description

The woman stands on her head, comfortably, with vines supporting her. Her hair dips into the waters of the unconscious, and her feet reach up to the super-conscious sky. She wears X-ray glasses to see what's normally unseen. The root of the lotus is unseen, but goes deep, a symbol, here, for the depth of her journey. The spiral on the snail's shell symbolizes growth and evolution.

Spiritual

Peace, surrender, and deep understanding are the essence of this highly spiritual card. Outwardly, the woman seems to be doing nothing, just hangin' there, but so much is going on. She's calmly turned inward and surrendered to the rhythms of nature and of life. She feels connected, and she sees everything in a new way.

Hangin' invites you to do the internal work necessary to gain a new vision. By letting your ego slip, you become aware of your connection to all of life, and you experience your true self. Drawing this card confirms your journey; you've come a long way and arrived at the point where you can no longer pretend to be anyone other than who you truly are.

Practical

You may be called to tackle a problem from a previously unrealized angle. Or put yourself in someone else's shoes and try to see their perspective.

Sometimes the Hangin' card may show up to comfort you, representing the peace that comes after difficulty. Or it may indicate the need for some quiet, reflective time.

DEATH

Death

Description

The woman in the Death card is featureless because she's no longer concerned with self. To ancient Egyptians, owls protected spirits as they passed from one world to another. The lotus is from the Buddhist tradition; symbolizing purity, the long stalk rises out of the muddy waters to produce a beautiful flower. And the butterfly shows transformation as it moves from caterpillar to spread its gorgeous wings.

Spiritual

Not to be feared—Death is a deeply spiritual card referring to ego death. If you're in the process of watching your ego's grip loosen, you know it can be scary, because you don't know what life will be like without it. But you're also aware of your expanding consciousness. My meditation teacher described it like this: Before, it's like you're looking at the sky through a straw. After, it's like you see the whole sky.

The Death card wants to assure you that what lies ahead is the connection to all of life—and its unbelievably beautiful! As your ego dies, duality dies, and you simply experience wholeness and connection.

Practical

Death means change. Habits and ways of thinking that no longer fit fade away. A relationship or a career that you can no longer maintain passes. The change could bring about a crisis, but trust that it's necessary. Often, something must die before something can be born.

Rarely, this card may point to physical death; as you know, you and everyone you love are governed by Mother Nature's laws.

FLOW

Flow

Description
This chick floats on the water, moving with the currents of life. Above, the sun represents the positivity of this card.

Spiritual
What a way to be! Flow's the state of being you experience when your inner world is calm and you've learned to flow with life—instead of resisting it. It's when the battle ceases and you welcome the experiences and feelings that come your way instead of grasping at them or pushing them away.

You've come to Flow because you no longer need to hold on to the illusion that you're the center of the Universe. As your ego's grip loosens, you move with the bigger picture of your life. In this relaxed and mature state, your true path opens up to you—and you walk with it!

Feeling part of this big, beautiful, expansive life energy is invigorating and, at the same time, it's peaceful and really secure. In Flow, you move through the world around you naturally, trusting yourself and life. How great is that?

Practical
Practically, Flow shows up in your reading to advise you to take what Buddhists call "the middle path," avoiding indulgence on the one hand and self-denial on the other.

Flow wants you to embrace the power of being calm. Through the state of calm, you access your intelligence and make good decisions. Sometimes, doing nothing is best. Doing nothing is doing something; it's a choice and in some cases a very wise one.

BOUND

Bound

Description

The woman in the Bound card is tied up, and the rain cloud overhead symbolizes her sorrow.

Spiritual

There may be unconscious thoughts, feelings, and attitudes that are keeping you bound, eating up your energy, and limiting your view. They may be surfacing to your consciousness and making you uncomfortable—but this discomfort is an important part of the process. The good news is: Bound has shown up to help you loosen the ropes and move freely!

You're being called to be aware of the limitations you've created for yourself. Do you hide from your power? Are you a perfectionist? Are you judging yourself and others? Just observing these restrictions helps the rope slip. The energy that was all bound up will start to be released, and you'll be able to use it to make new discoveries about yourself and move forward on your spiritual path.

This process requires intense self-examination. It takes courage to acknowledge parts of yourself that may seem undesirable to you. Untangling yourself from ingrained thoughts and behaviors takes humility and patience. Be kind to yourself through the process.

Practical

Are you feeling stuck and powerless? Bound reminds you that often your limitations are of your own making. Are you narrowly focused and in need of shifting to a larger view of your circumstances? If you're dealing with an addiction, Bound may be encouraging you to seek the help you need.

TOWER

Tower

Description

The tower is crumbling and a smiling woman flies away in the light being released. The lightning bolt represents how this dramatic change seems so sudden, yet it's been brewing for a while. The moon and the cloud speak to the mysterious quality the event holds—so much unconscious energy rising to the surface.

Spiritual

You have so much energy waiting to be released! The Bound card reminded you about the restrictions your defenses and ego impose—what an energy drain. Now the Tower card shows up to set you free. The card screams liberation! The lightning bolt represents insight that can come as a flash, destroying illusions and breaking up old ways of thinking and being. The old structure is crumbling and your true self is being released. This is an experience of profound, drastic spiritual transformation.

Practical

Tower is a high-energy card, and when it's pulled, it means change. Like the woman flying away Superman-style, it's time to move on!

Tower energy is a blessing if you're willing to accept the pain of letting go of what no longer works for you, no matter how familiar and comfortable it may seem—and trust life to lead the way forward.

You've changed and you're just not able to accept the constrictions of a crappy job, a bad relationship, or a self-defeating habit any more. What comes disguised as a loss may be the catalyst for liberating internal and external change—a chance to live a more authentic life.

STAR

Star

Description
The woman floats peacefully in the calm waters, blessed by the star shining above her.

Spiritual
Ah . . . take a moment to drink in this beautiful image: The woman rests in the vast, formless ocean. She doesn't need to do a thing—just be there, just float. She's connected to Source and has everything she needs. Star shows up in your reading to remind you: When your mind is calm and your heart is happy, you're connected, too. This peaceful, joyous place is always available, but often you'll become aware of it after a crisis—it's the calm after the storm.

As you grow in your spirituality, you'll live in this calm consciousness for longer periods of time. You'll feel a profound sense of safety, security, and freedom because you know that all is unfolding as it should. The storms of your life will dance over the surface of the water. Trust that your energy will always be renewed.

Practical
Star is the card of deep healing and wholeness. Drawing this card may point to a release of painful memories and negative feelings. Star wants you to listen to your inner voice and let it guide you to take care of yourself.

This card may also show up because it's a very creative time. You may be inspired to do something—and you'll have the confidence to do it! Star encourages you to follow your instincts, and pursue what brings deeper meaning and purpose to your life.

moon

moon

Description

With the moon above, the sun awaits the woman once she passes through the darkness. She wades through choppy waters surrounded by a lobster representing primitive emotion, a wolf representing wildness, a bat associated with night, and an octopus reminding you of the softness and flexibility required to face your fears.

Spiritual

There's some scary stuff lurking around inside of you, and Moon is asking you to let it rise to the surface; this requires a relaxed mind able to welcome unpleasant thoughts and feelings so they can be examined. Once acknowledged, your guilt and fear give up their hold on you, and you experience a profound freedom (that's the glory of the next card, Sun).

Moon doesn't offer the shining light of Star or the full light of Sun, but it's enough light to guide you through the tough times. Moon brings hope. And it asks for faith—faith that night will fade and the sun will return.

Practical

Moon is the card of deep feelings and primitive emotions. Fear is a biggie! Are you venturing out of your comfort zone, unsure of the outcome? Don't let your imagination wander into worst-case scenarios. Practice faith and follow your intuition.

Sometimes, Moon appears because you don't have all the information necessary to assess a situation or your vision has been clouded by miscommunication, rumors, or lies. Moon is telling you to wait until things become clearer before you act.

ſuη

ſuη

Description
A smiling woman jumps for joy under a brilliant sun!

Spiritual
The Moon card required bringing your fears into the light. Now that they're not creeping in the shadows, they're not so scary. You're not struggling against your fear or trying to avoid it through compulsive or escapist behavior. You feel a tremendous release of energy.

In this sunny state, you, everyone, and everything you encounter is beautiful—filled with Divine light! Your inner and outer worlds merge, and you flow through the experiences of your day. You see the crabby waiter in the same glowing light as you see the smiling friend.

Even challenging times aren't dark; you don't resist them because you're available to all your emotions and all the circumstances life brings you. You're innocent and wise at the same time, light of heart and deep in spirit.

Practical
Sun is about really good stuff: optimism, joy, and childlike wonder. It may be acknowledging the joy you feel or will be feeling. Or it may be giving you the green light on your relationship, the go-ahead on your project, or the thumbs up on your career move—letting you know success is in your future.

Or it could be reminding you to have fun. You may want to break free from your normal routine and walk in the park or call a friend you haven't talked with in a while. Go ahead, stop and smell the flowers!

REBORN

Reborn

Description
The chick in the Reborn card is emerging from her shell—brand new, reborn! She isn't fully out yet, but she knows there's no turning back now. The sun overhead blesses her.

Spiritual
The Universe is calling—and the purpose of Reborn is to take the call! This call comes from deep within you and invites you to fully live what some part of you has already accepted. Sun was about dissolving fear, what's left is Universal Truth. The Truth is: You're not an isolated individual; you and everyone and everything are connected, part of the Universe, pulsating with life!

Reborn is about just that—being reborn into this new consciousness. You and life merge—the ordinary and the eternal unite. As this mystical process unfolds, it's wondrous and a little scary; you haven't fully experienced this new way of being that comes with the Universe card, yet you have no desire to go back to your old way. At this point, you need faith. As you relax into this new way of being, your life takes on deeper meaning and you enjoy your newly expanded consciousness.

Practical
Practically, Reborn points to life changes; it could be a change in career, relationship, residence, or in any other area of your life where something doesn't seem to fit anymore. Reborn energy calls you to acknowledge you've changed; you've grown on the inside. Time to make your external life match your new internal one.

UNIVERSE

Universe

Description
The Universe chick floats in expanding space, surrounded by planets and stars. She moves to the rhythm of her hula hoop. The hula hoop is a circle that symbolizes eternity and motion.

Spiritual
You've integrated the lessons of the Tarot and arrived at enlightenment. It's a big deal and, paradoxically, it's not because it's your true nature, that was there all along; it's the nature of the Universe. It's an energy, and you embody that energy by letting go and expanding. You drop your tiny self-centered world and merge with the Universe, comfortable, secure, and truly at home.

There's no need to struggle because there's no "good" or "bad." You're always in the right place, at the right time, as you move through your experience because the center of the Universe is everywhere, and everywhere you go—there it is.

Just by being yourself, you help to liberate others. Once you've experienced the light of Universal Truth, there's no going back. You can dim the light by reverting to old habits, but the call to acknowledge and live in this consciousness is very loud and hard to ignore.

Practical
When Universe shows up in your reading, relating to practical matters, it's a blessing—assuring you all's well in the big picture that's sometimes hard to see. It's inviting you to step back and widen your view. It's time to relax and celebrate success and the feeling of completeness.

MINOR ARCANA DESCRIPTIONS AND MEANINGS

SUIT OF CREATE

The suit of Create embodies the powerful spark of human potential. Red, the color of blood—life itself—pulses through you and this suit. The paintbrush symbolizes your creativity. Create energy is expansive, optimistic, and on the move. This energy combines with your intellect and imagination to make projects and relationships happen.

Fire is Create's element—hot and sexy! Create cards remind you to connect deeply with every area of your life; love yourself and others, dive into your work, and play with passion. Experience your life, all of it—the joy and pain—and everything in between—with red-blooded courage!

Spiritually, Create cards call you to live your truth beyond the meditation room, out there in the world where everything is messy and in motion. Take the fire that burns within and channel it into what you care about.

Queen of Create

QUEEN OF CREATE

Description

The Queen wears her crown like a natural and holds her paintbrush with confidence. The rainbow symbolizes her creativity, and the rose symbolizes her beauty.

Meaning

Queen of Create uses her enormous energy to connect to the world and other people. People like her because she's honest and happy. She sees the best in others, but can easily navigate situations and set boundaries if needed.

Basically, she wants to have a good time, but far from being a hedonist, this woman doesn't go to extremes. She knows how to take care of herself. She enjoys her body and exercise and sex.

She's a natural at anything she decides to do. She has the ability to create a wonderful life for herself and contribute to the people around her. Her message to you is: Enjoy your life! Focus your energy into creating happiness and health!

Boss of Create

BOSS OF CREATE

Description
The boss's message is summed up on her button: Do it! From her paintbrush emanates a rainbow of creativity.

Meaning
Boss of Create takes creativity and enthusiasm and blends them with skill and willpower to turn her ideas into reality. She's passionate and not afraid to take a risk. If she fails at something, it doesn't keep her down; she learns from her mistakes and uses that knowledge to create her next success. Her abilities make her a natural leader and an excellent entrepreneur.

Do you have something you want to accomplish? Boss of Create is telling you: Do it! While no outcome is guaranteed, this energy is about being passionate enough to start and committed enough to see your project through the ups and downs it takes to arrive at success.

Teen of Create

TEEN OF CREATE

Description

Teen of Create is racing toward her next adventure with creative energy (symbolized by the rainbow) flowing from her paintbrush.

Meaning

Teen of Create is about physical, mental, and spiritual energy finding an outlet in the world. You're inspired and ready to make it happen! Now may be the time to move ahead on that business deal or take your relationship to the next level or jump on a plane and fly to your dream destination.

But there's also the possibility that your enthusiasm is preventing you from seeing the whole picture and making the plans needed to make your adventure successful. When this card appears in your reading, the message is usually move forward! But, depending on surrounding cards, you may want to prepare more before you do.

Child of Create

CHILD OF CREATE

Description
This imaginative kid is thinking about what to paint with her rainbow paintbrush, while the sun shines its blessings on her.

Meaning
Child of Create is eager to start a new project or begin a new relationship. She's playful in her approach and not afraid to make a mistake. When Child of Create appears in your reading, she's whispering in your ear: Take a chance; give it a try.

Have you always wanted to learn how to yodel? What's stopping you? Are you curious about someone new? Why not ask that person out? Do you want to dig those tap shoes out of the closet and dance? Go ahead! Connect with the innocent, curious part of yourself. Who knows where this playful energy will lead you?

Ace of Create

ACE OF CREATE

Description
Ace of Create shows a paintbrush dipped in green. The paintbrush symbolizes creative power, and green is the color of growth and new life. Passion is expressed in the red background.

Meaning
Ace of Create is bursting with creativity, strength, power, and passion—what a sexy card! And it's arrived in your reading to give you a thumbs up. It's time to take your tremendous creative potential and move it into action.

You feel that idea growing inside; it may have been there for a long time, gaining energy and harnessing your imagination. Or it may have come in a flash. Either way, that energy wants to find form in the material world—and you're the vehicle to make it happen. Take Ace of Create's blessing and go for it!

Two of Create

TWO OF CREATE

Description

A confident, imaginative woman contemplates future plans. The sun shines above her indicating success.

Meaning

The woman in Two of Create blends the imagination and confidence of Child of Create with adult know-how. She often shows up when you're in the planning stages of an endeavor. If you're thinking about starting something new, be confident—your ideas are great!

You're unique and what you have to present to the world is innovative. You've got inner strength and the ability to sense when the time is right for your vision to become reality. Because you're able to pitch your ideas with confidence, other people want to get on board and support you. Whether you're approaching investors for your start-up or asking your boss for a raise—you've got this!

Three of Create

THREE OF CREATE

Description
With one foot firmly on the ground, the woman in Three of Create takes the first step. She holds her plans in her hand, prepared for her new adventure.

Meaning
The woman in Three of Create takes care of business in a mature way, making plans and anticipating problems in advance, so she's prepared to deal with them should they come up. She's hardworking, active, and adventurous—always looking for new opportunities in business and in her personal life.

When Three of Create shows up in your reading, you're being called to take the first step forward in your endeavor. It's scary, but you can do it! You've checked out the situation and made the plan—time to put it into action.

Four of Create

FOUR OF CREATE

Description

A self-portrait is finished and framed by four paintbrushes. The smile on the woman's face and the happy face pin reflect the joy she feels.

Meaning

The woman in Four of Create is happy about her accomplishment, and she's shown up in your reading to remind you to take a moment to acknowledge your accomplishments. What have you completed? Cleaning the attic? A project at work? Raising a child? Maybe you completed your career and are retiring. Whatever you've done—congratulations!

Four of Create is a card of stability and abundance. Your efforts have paid off. You can afford to pause here—give yourself a pat on the back—and celebrate! Sometimes, the card is simply saying: You're finished here. It's time to move on to something new.

Five of Create

FIVE OF CREATE

Description

The women in Five of Create are using their paintbrushes to fight each other instead of using them to build something together.

Meaning

Feeling competitive? Maybe you want to compete in a marathon or a chess tournament. Zooming to the finish line or capturing your opponent's queen is fun. Maybe you're striving to win a promotion at work or the karaoke contest at the bar. That's cool—Five of Create encourages healthy competition.

But it warns against the unhealthy kind. Often pettiness and jealousy need to be looked at when you're competing in an unhealthy way. Own it if it's coming from you. If it's coming from someone else, be creative and try an alternative way of interacting, or remove yourself from the scene until things calm down.

Six of Create

SIX OF CREATE

Description

A smiling woman raises her trophy—the symbol of her victory!

Meaning

Six of Create means success in the public arena. The woman in this card has overcome whatever was necessary to reach her goal, and she's being acknowledged and rewarded. When you draw this card, it could mean a raise is coming your way, or there's going to be an article published about you. Maybe you're receiving an award for the volunteer work you've done. Congratulations—you deserve it!

Or Six of Create may be indicating that your efforts will be acknowledged in the future. In that case, hang in there—and have faith! Your novel can be published. That diploma can be yours. You can get that job. Whatever challenges come along, know that you can handle them.

Seven of Create

JEVEN OF CREATE

Description
Step by step, the woman scales the mountain.

Meaning
Yeah, what you're going through can be tough at times. There are plenty of challenges along the way, but you're not only up for them, you love them—because the challenges have become interesting, fun even. You've learned to love the process of climbing the mountain as much as you love reaching the top. You're on your way, so Seven of Create has shown up to acknowledge your climb and congratulate you on your attitude.

Or it might be reminding you to take care of yourself. You may have an inner conflict or a challenge in your environment that's making your life feel like an uphill battle. In that case, what do you need to do to make your life easier, more enjoyable?

Eight of Create

EIGHT OF CREATE

Description
A woman hurls her paintbrushes through the air. The sun above symbolizes energy and power.

Meaning
Eight of Create is a big burst of energy. It's about things happening—and fast! It's a time of action and usually indicates a good outcome. You may be making progress with a project, and it's nearing completion. Are you feeling energized? Are ideas and solutions coming easily?

Eight of Create is telling you to proceed confidently. But, depending on what other cards have shown up with it, it may suggest you're rushing into something or things are scattered. In that case, slow down and give it a little more time before you run to the bank to sign the papers or fly to Vegas to get married. Wait until things settle.

Nine of Create

NINE OF CREATE

Description
The storm is passing. The woman holds her paintbrush upright and looks to the future.

Meaning
Are you going through a rough patch? Is it changing you? The experiences life brings you, shape you. And you choose how. The woman in Nine of Create has shown up to tell you: Take the experience—no matter how painful—and use it to develop yourself.

Have you been betrayed? Then you've been given the opportunity to find compassion for yourself and the one who hurt you. Do you find yourself lonely? Then you've been given the opportunity to turn your loneliness into a rich inner and spiritual life. Everything is playing out as it should. As you love yourself through this, with your heart open, you heal and become even more beautiful.

Ten of Create

TEN OF CREATE

Description
A woman struggles under the weight that she carries on her back. A gray cloud follows her.

Meaning
Wow, what's weighing you down? Do you need to get organized? Would that make things easier? Do you have too many responsibilities, stuff you could delegate or eliminate? Don't be afraid to set boundaries, ask for help, or say no.

When you pull Ten of Create, you're being invited to go deeper and ask yourself what motivates you to overdo. Do you have a problem trusting others with tasks?

Are you trying to please someone, doing more than your share in the relationship because you're afraid of losing them? If you become aware of your motives, you can drop the load, liberate yourself—and even have some fun!

SUIT OF FEEL

Blue, the color of water, flows through this beautiful suit. Feel cards are about love and your connection to all of creation. They invite you into the realm of your heart and reveal the truth about your relationship to self, others, and all that's going on in your life.

Feel cards call you to honor your feelings as teachers and learn to tune in deeply, so you can hear the messages they bring to you. It takes courage to own your feelings—all of them—even the ones that aren't pleasant.

By calmly asking yourself what you're feeling, you turn nonverbal messages into words. And—as if by magic—the unconscious becomes conscious. Making your feelings comfortable is important; allow yourself to be sad or scared. Cultivate compassion for the feeling, and watch it melt away, leaving you with important insight into your situation.

Queen of Feel

QUEEN OF FEEL

Description

This queen is beautiful inside and out. Water, symbolizing feeling and the unconscious mind, flows from her crown and into her hand, becoming conscious and ready for her to put to use in her next creation.

Meaning

Queen of Feel is highly evolved and highly creative. Tuning into how she feels is her place of power. She brings consciousness to the watery realm of emotion—and lets her imagination soar! She has the ability to bring her ideas into reality, not solely by will, but through love.

A natural artist, she creates a beautiful life for herself and contributes to those around her. When you pull this card, know that you're an artist and your life is your creation. Trust yourself and your feelings. See and appreciate the beauty of this world.

Boss of Feel

BOSS OF FEEL

Description

The fish swimming behind Boss of Feel symbolize emotion and the ability to confidently go with the flow of life.

Meaning

Boss of Feel's heart and mind work together. Her emotional maturity brings stability to her relationships and business endeavors. And she brings a big boost of confidence to anyone feeling overwhelmed by their circumstances and emotions.

Boss of Feel believes in you. She's shown up in your reading to say: You have what it takes to handle whatever is going on in your life. So, if you need to break up with your partner, you can do it. If you need to be more patient with your partner, you can do that. Feeling afraid to set some boundaries with someone? Boss of Feel says: Hey, you're the boss!

Teen of Feel

TEEN OF FEEL

Description
This teen is young at heart, and her head is in the clouds.

Meaning
Teen of Feel's youthful enthusiasm can be fun and refreshing, but she doesn't always see clearly. Her head is in the clouds, full of fantasies and daydreams, and instead of owning her feelings, she has a habit of projecting them on other people. All this can result in poor judgment, confusion, and inaction.

When you pull Teen of Feel, you're being advised to enjoy your fantasies; you can use them to inspire your art, for example, or they can point to a longing in your soul. But don't get lost in them. Make sure you're connected to the reality of your life, so you can make good decisions and take appropriate action.

Child of Feel

CHILD OF FEEL

Description

Child of Feel is happy! The balloon symbolize her joy, the stars symbolizes her imagination, and the daisy symbolizes her innocence.

Meaning

There's great joy to be had in life, especially in your relationships—including the one you have with yourself! Child of Feel doesn't get bored because her imagination and ability to tune into her feelings contribute to a rich inner life. She enjoys the simple pleasures of kissing her loved one's cheek, petting her cat's back, and shaking her neighbor's hand.

She's here to tell you: It's not about the future, although a new relationship may be developing—it's about enjoying the here and now! Don't try to manipulate the outcome of a relationship; enjoy the people in your life, and allow relationships to unfold naturally.

Ace of Feel

ACE OF FEEL

Description
A red heart rests on a blue background; red symbolizes love and passion, and blue symbolizes emotion, in general.

Meaning
The suit of Feel deals in the realm of what you hold most dear, what gives your life meaning. It's about love, passion, and connection. Ace of Feel may arrive in your reading to point out the blessings of your relationships with family and friends or just to reassure you that all's going well. It's an optimistic card, and when you draw it during a rough time, it's message is simply: Take heart. The Universe always has your back, even when things are difficult, and you're feeling unsure of yourself.

Ace of Feel encourages you to seek out people who support you. But, mostly, it calls you to acknowledge whatever is going on with you, feel it fully, love yourself, and know that—all of your life—is beautiful, meaningful, and blessed.

Two of Feel

TWO OF FEEL

Description
A pregnant woman connects to her growing baby. Her yin-yang tattoo is a symbol of harmony and balance.

Meaning
Two of Feel is about harmony, love, and relationship. Drawing this card may indicate the beginning of a new relationship for you. It's a beautiful thing to want to get to know someone and to open up and want to be known.

The union may be with a lover or a friend or a child. Or it may be with someone who ends up just passing through your life. No matter how brief, the connection is valuable and meaningful.

This card can also be about your connection with a project that you're passionate about. Ever feel so completely absorbed in painting or writing or some other endeavor that time stands still, and you seem to abandon yourself? Sounds a lot like love, doesn't it?

Three of Feel

THREE OF FEEL

Description

Three friends are celebrating. It's a fun time with fancy drinks, party hats, and balloons.

Meaning

This card is all about happiness, shared experience—and celebration! The spiritual aspect manifests in recognizing your connection to other beings and the blessings they bring to your life. This appreciation is beyond the petty differences that can sometimes come between you. It's about loving your friends, warts and all—just the way you strive to love yourself.

Three of Feel may show up to nudge you to take a break from work and go have fun with your friends. Sometimes, this card appears in a reading to indicate cooperation with co-workers, family members, or any group effort where good will prevails. If you're joining a group, it's a good omen to get this card.

Four of Feel

FOUR OF FEEL

Description

The bored woman stares into space. The three hearts in front of her represent the status quo of her life, all neatly lined up: relationships, work, recreation. What she doesn't see is another heart floating overhead. It's come to her on wings like an angel—it's that magical and mysterious quality that's there when you look for it.

Meaning

Uninspired? Bored? Everything's okay, it's just that something is missing. What's missing is the magic, the force that can be easily forgotten, but must be acknowledged for you to truly feel inspired.

When you pull Four of Feel, you're being invited to look beyond the material and see the magic that's always hanging around, waiting for you to tune into it. Relax, refresh, and see with the eyes of a child.

Five of Feel

FIVE OF FEEL

Description

Out of five hearts, three are tipped over; that's the majority and it represents a profound loss and sometimes regret. The woman in Five of Feel is feeling the loss—deeply. The cloud represents sadness, yet the sun still shines.

Meaning

This card is about loss on some level, everything from the death of a loved one, to the loss of employment, to the loss of confidence. Whatever has happened it's profound and can be life-changing. When Five of Feel comes up in your reading, it's asking you to acknowledge your loss and take the time to feel it and heal from it.

A card of emotional maturity and intelligence, Five of Feel calls you to take responsibility if you caused the situation. Then, with wisdom, you can turn and face what's waiting for you—the two upright hearts that remain!

Six of Feel

SIX OF FEEL

Description

A woman approaches her childhood home with balloons in hand. A friendly sun shines overhead.

Meaning

Six of Feel is about traveling to that place of innocence that you felt as a child. You may remember being loved and cared for by a parent or a special bond you shared with a pet. Even if your childhood wasn't happy, this card invites you to remember something sweet from that time; it could be your natural sense of wonder, your appreciation of nature, or the joy of learning something new.

When this card comes in a reading, it means something feels good to you and indicates happiness and security. But if you're longing for and idealizing the past, it's reminding you that your power is here and now.

Seven of Feel

SEVEN OF FEEL

Description

The woman is on her phone, multitasking. She's thinking about a relationship, as indicated by the ring. She considers having a baby. Her thoughts go to something tragic (the skull) and then yummy (the cake). She fantasizes about a vacation, represented by the palm tree, and a money-making proposition, indicated by the bag of cash.

Meaning

Daydreaming is worthwhile because it reveals your desires, but getting stuck there is a drag. At some point, you need to choose a course of action. Choosing takes courage because often it means closing down another path, at least for a while. For example, choosing the vacation means you're putting off the job search.

Seven of Feel can also indicate confusion or deception. If someone or something seems weird, you might want to take a step back and get some perspective. Trust your intuition.

Eight of Feel

EIGHT OF FEEL

Description

The woman in this card is leaving her hearts behind her and moving on to higher awareness as symbolized by the mountain. Inner awareness and change are expressed by the eclipsed moon.

Meaning

Your current situation no longer fits your evolving soul. It takes a lot of courage to leave the known and move into the unknown, but the call of Eight of Feel comes from a deep place within that needs to be fulfilled.

If you're being called, you know that you have to listen! You know because it feels right. You feel still, calm, and sure. Other people aren't always aware of your inner development, and they may not understand what you want to do. Don't be swayed by their opinions. Do what's right for you.

Nine of Feel

NINE OF FEEL

Description
The woman sits cross-legged in an ample armchair, sipping tea. She's happy and content with life and grateful to be enjoying its little pleasures. The daisy on her knee patch is a symbol of simplicity.

Meaning
Nine of Feel is a cozy card. It's about making yourself comfortable on all levels: physically, spiritually, and emotionally. When you tune into Nine of Feel, life gets easier because you're using your energy to serve yourself well and let things fall into place.

Nine of Feel may be pointing to your comfort with a person or a project. Or it may be asking you: How can you make yourself more comfortable? Do you need help with something? Would you like to take some time off?

Ten of Feel

TEΠ OF FEEL

Description

The women in this card are blessed to be together. They know it and they celebrate it. Their embrace is warm and they're happy and secure in their home as hearts float through the sky above them.

Meaning

Ten of Feel is a happy card! It's about knowing what is valuable in your life and seeing the goodness around you. It can express your delight in nature, your appreciation of art, or the enjoyment found in your favorite hobby. But, often, it's about the joy found in relationships with friends and family and spouses and lovers.

It's about being happy in your home, the safe place where you live, and remembering that your real home is inside of you. All the joy you need can be found in your own heart.

SUIT OF THINK

The suit of Think is represented by yellow, the color of mental energy. This suit is about the power of your mind. You're rational and clever and you're flexible and creative and you have the ability to think outside the box.

Think also acknowledges your problems caused by over-thinking, negative thinking, and conflicting ideas. Think's element is air, and it's always in motion. A cool breeze can shift into a storm. This storm can erupt into arguments or swirl around creating anxiety. Sometimes, conflicting ideas paralyze a person, leaving her unable to make a critical decision.

Think energy works best when combined with the energies of the other suits. Earth takes the ideas out of your head and anchors them into reality. Create energy brings much-needed optimism. And Feel energy is really great—head and heart working together—that's the ultimate combination!

Queen of Think

QUEEN OF THINK

Description

Queen of Think scrutinizes her world. Her crown indicates her stature and the light bulb symbolizes her intelligence.

Meaning

This woman has a sharp mind that is informed through her feelings, so she usually accurately assesses the situation. She'll cut to the heart of the matter and articulate it in a take-no-prisoners fashion. When you pull this card, you may need to look deeper at events or people in your life—and you may need to speak your mind.

Do you need to heal from betrayal or other disappointments? Queen of Think is telling you: You've got the power to turn pain into wisdom.

Or you may need to examine the thoughts you have about others and yourself. Are you being too harsh? Do you need to tune your inner dialogue to a less critical station?

Boss of Think

BOSS OF THINK

Description
Boss of Think is sharp (symbolized by the light bulb) and so full of ideas lightening radiates from her head. Her "can do" button sums up her attitude.

Meaning
Her ideas are brilliant, but she doesn't rush to implement them. She does the research required before she begins. People trust her because she's a natural leader who's gained a reputation for being honest and fair.

Boss of Think is telling you: You can handle the task in front of you. She encourages you to take the steps necessary to optimize your chances for success. Research, talk to others in your field, practice your presentation to the point where you feel confident, and examine your motives. Do you want everyone involved to feel good about the transaction?

Teen of Think

TEEN OF THINK

Description
This teen has an idea—and she's racing full speed ahead with it.

Meaning
Wow! You've got a great idea and you're inspired to act on it. Or you may need to get out of a situation or away from another person—fast. Depending on the other cards in the spread, that may be the thing to do.

But it's also possible you need to slow down, take a look around, and reassess your situation because Teen of Think is known to be impulsive sometimes.

Sometimes the right thing to do is nothing—just wait for more information or better timing or let things work out naturally. Waiting isn't always comfortable, but in that stillness, you can gain perspective and strength before you make your next move.

Child of Think

CHILD OF THINK

Description

This happy, curious child points to her idea, symbolized by the light bulb.

Meaning

Children see the world in a fresh way. Child of Think is about the simple delight of having a mind. It's about the surprise, joy, and clarity of the ah-ha moment. You've been seeing things one way—then suddenly a light bulb in your brain turns on to give you a new way to look at it!

Who knows what will come of it? This shift may lead to a new business plan, a path to improving a relationship, or the ability to untangle yourself from an unwanted habit. This childlike way of seeing can bring you deeper into your spirituality. By letting go of old, rigid ideas, you embrace a new, more relaxed, and creative mind.

Ace of Think

ACE OF THINK

Description

A light bulb symbolizes thoughts, ideas, and sudden realizations. The background color is yellow, associated with intelligence.

Meaning

The suit of Think is intelligent and analytical and sometimes in conflict—after all, thoughts can clash. But Ace of Think represents the best the suit has to offer: clarity, perception, and decisiveness.

Drawing this card can point to a new idea, a spark of realization, or insight brought to a baffling situation. It may be telling you to think creatively or look at a problem from a new angle. If you're having an argument, it may challenge you to try to see the other person's point of view.

Ace of Think is exciting and can lead to adventure and discovery, but remember: Thinking works best when it's in tune with feeling.

Two of Think

TWO OF THINK

Description
The woman shrugs her shoulders, unable to decide.

Meaning
Do you need to say yes or no to someone or something? Could there be a third option? Maybe part of you wants to tell someone off, and another part of you wants to run and hide, and you're feeling tense and stuck. Two of Think is calling you to relax and open up to seeing the bigger picture.

This requires stepping back and putting a little space between you and the issue at hand. A long hot bath or a walk in the park could bring about the shift needed. Or you can simply call on the Divine to direct you. The Divine is always waiting to support you. You simply need to ask and calm yourself so you can receive the answer.

Three of Think

THREE OF THINK

Description

The sad woman stands with her arms across her chest, cutting herself off from her feelings. On her arm is a broken heart tattoo.

Meaning

Pain is part of life. You can try to push it away by denying it or distracting yourself from it, but it's still there, waiting to be acknowledged. When Three of Think shows up, it's calling you to open up to your feelings, including the ones you don't necessarily like or want to experience.

Through this process, you acknowledge your humanity, and you honor life by embracing it just the way it is. It's hard to hear during a rough time, but the Universe always has your back. You'll get through this. So, go ahead and cry if you need to, and trust it'll get better.

Four of Think

FOUR OF THINK

Description
The woman is curled up, sleeping peacefully. An owl, symbolizing wisdom, watches over her.

Meaning
Four of Think is about self-care, especially the need for quiet and rest. Is your mind running on overdrive? Is busyness taking a toll? When you draw this card, it's calling you to tune into how you're feeling and do what's best for you. This could be a long lunch, an afternoon nap, or a much-needed vacation. Or it may indicate the need to pull back from a situation or relationship that's uncomfortable or draining your energy.

Above all, this card celebrates wisdom, represented by the owl in the painting. Sometimes doing nothing is wise. Just let it be. Clear your mind. Give your problems to the Universe while you take a mental break.

Five of Think

FIVE OF THINK

Description

The women in this card are hurling light bulbs at each other. The light bulbs stand for attitudes and ideas.

Meaning

Five of Think is about opposing ideas and conflict. Not seeing eye-to-eye with your coworker? Maybe your landlord is in no rush to fix that leak you think is an urgent matter. You see it one way, and they see it another way.

Five of Think is here to tell you that conflict is part of life. It's reminding you to take the high road while taking care of yourself. Instead of hurling insults, try to be diplomatic. If that doesn't work, you may need to let go of a relationship or even call a lawyer. You can handle it—just remember to love yourself through the process (it'll help you be less fearful).

Six of Think

SIX OF THINK

Description

The woman walks her path. The baggage she carries isn't heavy because she isn't overthinking. The light bulbs illuminate her way, and the sun shines its blessings on her. The cloud acknowledges her sadness about leaving, while the happy face reflects her feelings about the future.

Meaning

There is quiet dignity in Six of Think. If it's referring to your spiritual path, the way ahead is relatively smooth. You know growth requires sacrifice and you take it in stride.

In practical matters, you might be moving on, leaving a relationship or a job or a place behind that no longer suits you. You're aware of the loss but wise enough to know it's simply time to go. As you feel the sadness of leaving, you move forward, knowing you're doing the right thing.

Seven of Think

SEVEN OF THINK

Description

The woman grabs her stuff and sneaks out the window.

Meaning

What's going on here? Something isn't right. Is this woman fleeing a relationship? Is she skipping out on the rent? Or is she robbing the house? Are you being less than honest with yourself? Are you being less than honest with someone else? Or is someone being dishonest with you?

If you need to own up to something you've done, now is the time to do it. If something is off in your relationship, now is the time to work it out or move on.

Seven of Think can also indicate a need to make a radical change in your life. You may need to go your own way, even if others don't understand, and you're a little unsure yourself.

Eight of Think

EIGHT OF THINK

Description
Eight light bulbs, representing her thoughts, are closing in on a distressed woman.

Meaning
The woman in Eight of Think is obviously in a really bad place. She's the victim of her own mind! Her negative thinking may be rooted in unhealthy patterns going back to childhood or limiting and shameful messages from society that she's internalized.

Her negative thoughts can result in obsession, depression, and isolation. When you pull Eight of Think, you're being asked to acknowledge that even if your distress is being caused by your circumstances—you can choose how to respond. You may want to seek help; with love and support, you can find the courage to face your problems in a healthy way and create a mind full of thoughts that reflect your true worth.

Nine of Think

NINE OF THINK

Description

A grieving woman sits in bed. Her cat and her quilt provide comfort.

Meaning

The woman in Nine of Think is in so much pain that she's retreated to bed. She feels crushed, but not hopeless. You may have pulled this card because something tragic has happened, like the death of a loved one or the end of an important job. You may be overwhelmed by an eviction notice or the diagnosis of a disease. Whatever the cause of your crisis, hope is not lost.

Your ability to grieve is proof that you're intact as a human being, able to react to your situation. And you are not alone; help is available to you.

Ten of Think

TEN OF THINK

Description
The woman lies on the floor, defeated. All the light bulbs are cracked and broken, but through the window, the sun is creeping into the picture.

Meaning
The good news is: The worst is over. The bulbs may be cracked and even broken, but the sun still shines, if you look for it. When you pull Ten of Think, take heart. Things may have gone south, but the cycle of life continues, and, when you reach the lowest point, things can only go up.

You'll get up, too. You'll dust yourself off, take what you've learned from the experience, and move on. It's no time for self-pity or indulging in your agony. Feel what you need to feel and gather your strength—because soon a new cycle will begin.

SUIT OF EARTH

Brown, like the earth, this suit involves nature, work, health, money, and all the down-to-earth stuff that makes up your daily life. This may seem humble and even a little mundane compared to the other suits, but remember: There's magic in the mundane. The paradox involves seeing what's just under the surface of your experience.

The word "grounded" sounds like it comes from the earth; it means being present and okay, no matter what's going on around you. By being grounded, you experience the spiritual. Because the world of nature is denser than the spiritual, it allows you to connect to the Divine without being overwhelmed by it.

Your body is beautiful, and it has tremendous knowledge. Through work you find meaning and community. Through nature you find healing and peace. The suit of Earth represents the stuff of life!

Queen of Earth

QUEEN OF EARTH

Description

Queen of Earth holds the world lovingly, and from her crown grows a flower. She's successful, practical, and knows how to enjoy life.

Meaning

Queen of Earth moves successfully through the world. She thrives at business because of her no-nonsense attitude, and she loves to share her material wealth with others. She knows how to take care of herself and everything in her realm.

When she shows up in your reading, she's urging you to get comfortable in your life, to create balance with work and pleasure. She wants you to take care of yourself and be practical. Would making time to go to the gym make your body feel better? Would a walk in the park relax your mind? Would saving some money for a rainy day add to your sense of security?

Boss of Earth

BOSS OF EARTH

Description

A laurel wreath symbolizes Boss of Earth's success. She carries the world easily on her shoulder and her pin says: Got this.

Meaning

Boss of Earth has been there and done that and knows how to handle whatever comes up with a calm head and a steady hand. From daily matters to big life maneuvers, she has the ability to succeed; she's as comfortable planning a child's party as she is planning the next step in her career. She works hard, is practical, and learns from experience. She enjoys her success and all that comes with it without being showy or indulgent.

When she arrives in your reading, she may be pointing to a prosperous business deal. If there's a challenge, remember: You've got this! Be confident and do what needs to be done.

Teen of Earth

TEEN OF EARTH

Description

A teenager struggles under the weight of the world she carries on her back.

Meaning

Teen of Earth is serious beyond her years. And she's carrying the weight of the world! She works hard, but instead of enjoying herself, she feels weighed down by her responsibilities. Because she hasn't learned to say no, others often lean on her. And worse yet, what she works so hard to accomplish and acquire leaves her feeling empty and unsatisfied.

This card may be acknowledging your hard work or it may be telling you hard work is necessary. But, often, you're being warned about burn out. Try to see beyond your day-to-day responsibilities and tune into your feelings; make time for yourself, and trust you'll be guided to what makes you happy.

Child of Earth

CHILD OF EARTH

Description
A child contemplates the world. Mountains in the background symbolize awareness and the river of imagination flows through this card.

Meaning
Child of Earth may have shown up to share your enthusiasm about a new project or idea. But often she appears with the gift of study and work.

Work is a big part of your life, and whether that work is school, raising children, a career, or a volunteer position, Child of Earth is here to remind you of the importance and satisfaction of a job well done.

This simple, honest energy isn't about getting recognition or a salary bump: It's about applying interest, imagination, and creativity to what you're spending your time doing. You're being called to get back to basics and recognize the Divine in your daily activities.

Ace of Earth

ACE OF EARTH

Description

The world floats on a brown background—very earthy.

Meaning

Ace of Earth represents the gifts of health and security. Drawing this card points to success and stability in all areas of life, including financial success. It represents the earthiness of the suit, yet it's here to remind you to see beyond the physical and into the spiritual manifested in the material world.

When you draw this card, you're being called to recognize the magic inherent in all you encounter. It's there in the simplest of interactions with others, the delight of your body, the bird on the windowsill, and the cream swirling in your coffee. By being present—grounding yourself on planet earth—you experience the beauty of Ace of Earth.

Two of Earth

TWO OF EARTH

Description

A woman juggles two worlds.

Meaning

Is the woman juggling the worlds trying to achieve balance in her life? Or is she juggling for fun? Could it be both?

Two of Earth might have shown up in your reading to remind you to make room for both fun and work. Or it could be reminding you to balance family obligations and self-care. Isn't always easy, right? Sometimes, an area of your life calls for extra attention. Be conscious of what's going on so you don't let yourself get burned out.

You may be called to slow down and focus—it's so easy to get distracted through multitasking. Perhaps a decision needs to be made. Whatever the case, Two of Earth wants you to relax and be flexible.

Three of Earth

THREE OF EARTH

Description
The construction worker is hard at work. The shaking hands symbolize her cooperation and connection with others.

Meaning
Three of Earth arrives in your reading to remind you of the inner growth that's occurring through your relationship with work and your relationships with your coworkers. Through work, you gain skill and confidence and you contribute to society.

If you're going through a hard time at work or feeling burned out, this card is asking you to focus on the bigger picture and see the value in what you're doing. If you're in an unsupportive work environment, you're being called to get in touch with what work means to you in order to make a decision about how to move forward.

Four of Earth

FOUR OF EARTH

Description

The four worlds sit squarely in this woman's wheelbarrow, symbolizing her solid financial situation. The watering can symbolizes the care she's put in to achieving it. And the sun overhead blesses her.

Meaning

The woman in Four of Earth is levelheaded and practical. She has created financial security for herself and her family—and she's letting you know you have the power to do the same. Her achievement is realized by carefully tending to her business and avoiding unnecessary drama.

If you're wondering about your financial future, this is a great card to draw. It also points to stability in other areas of life, like relationships, health, and well-being. Remember: The key, here, is nothing fancy—just solid planning, hard work, and the maturity to see things through.

Five of Earth

FIVE OF EARTH

Description

The card shows five worlds on the outside of a window and a woman, on the other side, in a house that's in disrepair. She's cut off from what she needs, and she feels isolated and deprived. Yet, the tattoo on her shoulder reads "faith."

Meaning

Five of Earth is about going through a hard time. You may be having money problems or experiencing a health crisis or you may be ending a relationship that was dear to you. Although this card acknowledges the sadness and loss you feel, it conveys another message too: faith.

Faith in action is about sitting in your uncomfortable circumstance with acceptance in your heart and having confidence that the Universe will see you through it. In the stillness that comes, you'll find the comfort you need.

Six of Earth

SIX OF EARTH

Description
Between the giving sun and the receiving moon, the woman holds a bowl of worlds. Has she just received it or is she about to give it away?

Meaning
To truly give, you can't expect anything in return. And to truly receive, you can't feel indebted to the giver. Sounds easy, but have you ever regretted giving a gift to someone? Maybe it was the gift of friendship. Maybe your gift wasn't appreciated in the way that you wanted it to be. And maybe you received something and felt weird about it because you sensed that it came with strings.

The Six of Earth is saying: Give what you can give without expectations. And take what is appropriate. It may also be asking you to take a look at your relationships. Is there a power imbalance somewhere?

Seven of Earth

SEVEN OF EARTH

Description

This woman's project has matured, symbolized by the blooming roses. She's taking a well-deserved vacation.

Meaning

Maybe your relationship or project is at a point where you can just kick back a little and enjoy. For example, when a child has matured, you can relax and relate in a different way. Or when your company is running smoothly, requiring less oversight and maintenance, you can afford to take some time off.

Seven of Earth may be pointing to a time of evaluation. You can look at what you've accomplished and decide if you're satisfied or want to make a few changes. For example, when you finish your novel, you might be wondering if you want to do another round of editing or if it's time to send it to your editor and start something new.

Eight of Earth

EIGHT OF EARTH

Description

This woman is creating her masterpiece. The suit of Earth deals with work and Eight of Earth expresses mastery in this arena.

Meaning

Is it time to take your project or your skills to the next level? It requires patience and attention to detail to become a master at your craft. You're working to produce something of value for yourself and your community. No outward glory is needed because the satisfaction is in the work itself.

Your work may be crafting a beautiful table or writing an elegant essay or raising a well-adjusted child. Whatever you're doing—feel good about it—and don't let perfectionism get in the way. Eight of Earth might also be acknowledging that you've reached a level of mastery, and it's time to look for a new challenge.

Nine of Earth

NINE OF EARTH

Description

Nine of Earth depicts the accomplishment of living life well. The woman's graduation cap symbolizes her knowledge of self. The garden that surrounds her blooms with the beauty and sweetness she's created, and the sun above blesses her.

Meaning

Nine of Earth energy isn't about impressing others or worldly achievement; it's about creating an authentic life that reflects solid values and right action. This card reminds you that true success is about how you feel about how you're handling the challenges of your life, regardless of your circumstances. A woman living in a trailer may have a richer inner life than a woman living in a mansion. Drawing this card reminds you of your true value and helps you realize the limits of materialism.

Ten of Earth

TEN OF EARTH

Description

The sun is shining, and a sack of money and a cornucopia of fruit, symbolizing material abundance, flank the woman in the Ten of Earth.

Meaning

The woman in this card has achieved more than security; she's gathered material wealth that supplies her with options in her life. She may be able to enrich herself with travel or buy a house or put money away for retirement. And she may be able to afford to help a friend or family member.

When you draw this card, be grateful for your prosperity and all it allows you to do. If you're contemplating a business opportunity, drawing Ten of Earth is a good omen. It can also point to stability in relationships and a good home life.

CLOSING THOUGHTS

So much beauty, wisdom, and spiritual knowledge has been handed down through countless Tarot decks, going all the way back to medieval times. I'm humbled to be adding my contribution, and I'm really happy that you're open to the messages that *Hip Chick Tarot* has for you. By reading the cards, we are all keeping the tradition alive for future generations.

May you be blessed with insight and happiness.

ACKNOWLEDGMENTS

I'd like to acknowledge all the people I have read for and all the readers who have read for me over the years. A few gifted readers stand out, especially, Emerald Stara. Your insight and love continues to help me on my path. And a big thanks to Dinah Roseberry, my editor. You believed in *Hip Chick Tarot* when it was just an idea, and now—thanks to you—it's real!